Grandma, Teach Me to Pray

Barbara A. Jones

This book is a work of non-fiction. Unless otherwise noted, the author and the publisher make no explicit guarantees as to the accuracy of the information contained in this book and in some cases, names of people and places have been altered to protect their privacy.

WestBow Press books may be ordered through booksellers or by contacting:

WestBow Press
A Division of Thomas Nelson & Zondervan
1663 Liberty Drive
Bloomington, IN 47403
www.westbowpress.com
844-714-3454

Because of the dynamic nature of the Internet, any web addresses or links contained in this book may have changed since publication and may no longer be valid. The views expressed in this work are solely those of the author and do not necessarily reflect the views of the publisher, and the publisher hereby disclaims any responsibility for them.

Any people depicted in stock imagery provided by Getty Images are models, and such images are being used for illustrative purposes only.
Certain stock imagery © Getty Images.

Interior Image Credit: Chad Thompson

Scriptures taken from the Holy Bible, New International Version®, NIV®. Copyright © 1973, 1978, 1984, 2011 by Biblica, Inc.™ Used by permission of Zondervan. All rights reserved worldwide. www.zondervan.com The "NIV" and "New International Version" are trademarks registered in the United States Patent and Trademark Office by Biblica, Inc.®

ISBN: 978-1-6642-1723-2 (sc)
ISBN: 978-1-6642-1724-9 (e)

Library of Congress Control Number: 2020925400

Print information available on the last page.

WestBow Press rev. date: 01/07/2021

WestBow
PRESS®
A DIVISION OF THOMAS NELSON
& ZONDERVAN

Grandma, Teach Me to Pray

Mornings started in my house with the sound of prayer vibrating through the halls by my grandma. I used to listen to my grandma pray in the mornings with her prayer partner and thought this was something that only older people did. They would take turns calling one another in the mornings. She later taught me that prayer is communicating with God at any age.

I came to realize that prayer was something that young and old should do. The coronavirus taught me just how much.

I was a senior in high school and excited about my senior year, senior day, prom, and graduation! I had already picked out the colors for my dress and knew the accessories that I would be wearing. I was college bound and positioned to graduate as class salutatorian! That Wendell Jefferson edged me out with a 4.0 GPA. I still think my guidance counselor miscalculated my GPA by half a point!

The buzz was we would be closing school for a couple weeks to give time for the rooms to be sanitized. My friends and I thought we'd be back to school in time for senior day. When we left school on March 13, 2020, we laughed and said, "See ya later." A few weeks later, the superintendent reported that public schools would remain closed until May 15 because deaths from the coronavirus pandemic continued to rise in the state. What did all this mean? Schools closed until May 15 and people dying. It's all hard to wrap my mind around. No, this could not be happening! Not attending prom I could handle, but not returning to school and graduating—now that bothered me.

Then it was reported that public schools would remain closed through the end of the academic year. Our schools were among forty-four other states that announced they had canceled in-person classes for the remainder of the academic calendar. Ugh! Was this a dream?

Switching to online learning would be trouble for me. I heard on the news about students who didn't have home Wi-Fi. I was one of those students. I didn't even own a laptop. I was waiting for the laptop to be issued from school. Yes, my mother worked. She was a single mother raising three hardheads and making ends meet the best she could. How was I going to complete my assignments? I had worked so hard for this moment, did everything that I needed to do; I scored 1210 on my SAT but wanted to take it again to improve my score. Now that wasn't going to happen. I screamed, *"Oh God, how could this be happening?"*

My grandma's room was next to mine, and she must've heard me. She knocked on my door. I told her to come in. She said, "I heard you asking God how this could be happening. What you need to do is ask the good Lord to help you to pray!"

I laughed and said, "Prayer is for old people."

She said, "That's what's wrong with young people. You think prayer is only for 'older' people. By the time God gets finished with us, we'll all be praying."

It just seemed like nothing was going right. My mother was now working from home, stores were closed, hair and nail salons were closed, restaurants were offering only curbside service, six-foot distancing was everywhere, and there was no inside church service. That's where I saw my friends— at church! Now we had to use YouTube, Zoom, FaceTime, WhatsApp, Instagram, and other social media platforms. We had to wear face masks and gloves and spray Lysol, and I still didn't know about prom or graduation.

I asked my grandma, "Where is God in this?"

She told me about Paul and what he wrote in Philippians 4:6. "Do not be anxious about anything, but in every situation, by prayer and petition, with thanksgiving present your requests to God." I asked her what that meant, and she said, "Believers should not be fearful about things that are happening in their lives. We should pray to God about *everything* that is going on in our lives. God has all power and authority and is in control of every situation—the good, bad, and in-between. God is listening and will answer." I asked her, "If He's listening, why is this happening?"

It's interesting that all the social media platforms that the older generation said we were spending too much time using are now the primary resources to stay connected.

That was the least of my worries. Without a laptop, I wouldn't be able to access my school assignments. In school I was able to use the laptop provided. It was just for in-school use, and without internet, it didn't matter if I had a laptop or not. What was I going to do? My mother was already doing all she could for me and my brothers. I couldn't ask her to buy me a laptop, knowing my brother needed one too. My younger brother didn't need one. After all he, was in kindergarten. I asked, "God, what am I going to do?"

Being home did have its advantages. I was able to spend time with my grandma, which was nice. I peeped in her room and saw her reading the Bible and overheard her talking to someone. After she finished talking, I knocked on the door and asked her if she was on the phone. She said, "No, child, I was talking with the Lord. He and I have had some good conversations lately. Ever since this coronavirus situation came, it reminds me of Noah in the ark in Genesis 7. That's what I was reading."

I didn't really understand what that meant, so I asked my grandma, "What do you and God talk about, and do you have a special dialogue?"

She said, "We talk about everything. Just like you talk with your friends, you can talk to God." In young adult church, the minister says something like, "You can tell God what's going on, but He already knows." If He knows, why did I have to tell Him? It didn't make sense.

We were sitting down for dinner, and my friend texted me that she heard they didn't know when or if we would have a prom, not to mention an in-person graduation. She said it was on the news! I started to cry, and my grandmother asked what was wrong. I said, "What isn't wrong? Coronavirus is messing up everything. No senior day, no prom, no graduation, no laptop, no internet. Why doesn't God fix this?"

By this time, my mother was in the dining room and slammed the pan down on the table. She said, "What is the matter with you? Everybody has something that they're dealing with. All I hear from you is 'Why is this happening to me?'"

This was the first time my mom showed any emotions. She normally held it all together. I never thought my mother also might be feeling the same kind of way. After all, she had been working from home for several weeks and wasn't getting full pay.

I was hanging out in my room after dinner, and my grandma came to see me. She said, "Kim, it's time that you learned to pray."

I said, "Are you serious? Praying is for old people."

She reminded me, "Kim, you used to pray when you were younger. Not sure what happened to you."

I started to cry and said, "Everything seems to be falling apart. Where did coronavirus come from? It has changed our lives. People are dying, and my friend told me that her grandma was sick with the coronavirus and was in the hospital." I didn't want that to happen to my grandma. "Grandma, what is going on in the world? Everything seems to be going in the opposite direction. If God already knows what is going on, why doesn't He just fix it? Why do we have to pray?"

My grandma said, "Come over here, girl. Let me talk to ya."

I love those moments with my grandma, laying my head in her lap as she rubs my back. "We serve a God who is in control of everything. He knows all and sees all. Isaiah 45:6–7: 'He ordained this would happen before it did.' Baby girl [I loved it when she called me that], He knew you before you were born [Jeremiah 1:5] and your momma, brothers, and even me!"

When Grandma said that, I asked, "How old is God?" She laughed and said, "Baby girl, Moses said that God was before the mountains and before the earth was formed. [Psalm 90:2]. He is certainly older than I am. Now don't mind how old God is. All we need to know is that He's taking care of us" (Hebrews 13:5–6).

I then sat up and said, "Grandma, can you *teach me to pray?* I was beginning to feel if praying will help get things back in line, let's do it!"

Grandma explained to me that praying is a conversation with God. There is no right or wrong way—sorta like talking to my friends. You just tell Him how you feel, but don't try to outpray others. Just be yourself (Matthew 6:5). To make it easier, use the ACTS method of Christian prayer.

- Adoration: give God praise and honor for who He is.
- Confession of our sin: we need His forgiveness.
- Thanksgiving: remember the grace and mercy God has shown toward us.
- Supplication or petition: bringing our requests for the needs of others and ourselves to God.

My grandma told me, "If it makes it easier, write your prayers down before you lift them to God. After all, they're your prayers!"

I said, "That's silly, but you know what? I'm gonna do it."

Later that evening, I was DM-ed by my friend, and she was really sad about her grandma.

She told me that because of her age and other medical issues, it would be harder for her to get over the coronavirus. I felt sad, thought about my conversation with my grandma, and told her to pray for her grandma to get better. She DM-ed me back and said, "Pray? You okay?"

I said, "I had this conversation with my grandma about all the things going on in the world: social injustice, police brutality, hunger, coronavirus, and what I was feeling, and she said I needed to pray. If prayer is the answer and will make things better, I'm willing to give it a try. After all, God hears us (1 John 5:14–15)."

Before I went to bed, I heard my grandma praying. This one was a little different. I wasn't being nosy or anything, but I was standing outside her door. I just needed to hear how she did it! I heard her say, "God, help my baby girl start that conversation with You. Teach her to pray, God."

I felt something inside me tingle. I don't know what it was, but I felt I could do this. I tried that ACTS prayer. I'm not sure how well I did, but I tried. I heard my grandma saying, "No right or wrong way to pray." Something in me that night gave me power to pray.

Dear God,

It's me, Kim. You are awesome, You are great, and I honor You in everything.

- A: Forgive me for my sins and for not always being respectful to my mom. I'm sorry I talked back when she asked me to do something.
- C: I thank You for my grandma, my mom, brothers, and friends.
- T: Now I ask that You help Ms. Rose get well.
- S: Help this coronavirus to go away, and return us to school to graduate. And until then, help me to get Wi-Fi so I may use my laptop.

In Jesus's name, amen!

This was the beginning of regular conversations with God, and it felt good. I told my grandma that I followed her advice on prayer (ACTS) and it worked. She said, "Yes, I've heard you."

We laughed and hugged each other.

The next day, my mother got the call from school that my laptop was ready, but that was only part of the problem. We still had no internet. We picked up the laptop, and my mom decided to see if she could work extra hours to get additional coins to pay for Wi-Fi. She wasn't even working forty hours.

A few weeks passed and my friend's grandma had recovered enough to go home. She still required care, but she was much better than when she had been in the hospital. Coronavirus was still at its peak; my mom didn't get any additional hours, but I was watching the news and heard all the libraries were offering free Wi-Fi internet to persons who had their own devices like laptops, iPads, and so forth. This was great news. God was answering some of my prayers. What I learned was how to even accept the prayers that didn't go my way (1 Thessalonians 5:16–18).

By now several weeks had passed. My mom was able to drive to the nearby library and I was able to sit in the car at the library and work on my assignments. Still no news about graduation. As it turned out, everyone who was cleared to graduate, was advised to pick up their cap and gown from school. It was strange being in school and not being able to see the faces of others. We each had on mask and all you could see were the eyes. We recognized each other by our eyes and it really felt good.

A few weeks had past and still no word on graduation. Later that day, while sitting around the house, my mother told me to put on my cap and gown. Graduation may be postponed, but they didn't stop us from having an honoring ceremony. I got excited thinking that I was going to finally have that chance to walk, even if it was across the backyard.

As it turned out, my mother and grandma, arranged with the school, an honoring ceremony at home for me and my closest friends, not more than a total of ten. We put on our caps and gowns and heard the graduation music "Pomp and Circumstance." A voice from the backyard said, "All rise to welcome our graduates." We marched outside, and to our surprise, the yard was decorated to include a stage. They played "Lift Every Voice and Sing," played former President Obama's graduation speech, and called our names, and we received certificates that said, "Diploma will follow." The graduates moved their tassels to the left, and we were officially 2020 graduates! We tossed our caps in the air.

We all were happy! It may not have been in the college arena, or even with a crowd of people, but it sure felt good.

I started to cry, and my grandma said, "What's the matter?"

I said, "I'm so glad I learned how to pray. Thanks for teaching me how to ACTS."

She said, "What you talking about, baby girl?"

I said, "I followed the ACTS method of praying. God does answer prayer. You just need to look closely. Come on now. Let's take a selfie!"

Printed in the United States
By Bookmasters